MOUNT PLEASANT

We are always learning about the planets, the stars, and what lies beyond. It is fun to search the night skies for planets and stars from our planet Earth.

MORE ABOUT OUR NINE PLANETS

MERCURY

Mercury, which is bigger than Earth's moon, has a core of iron.

VENUS

Venus rotates in the opposite direction of the other eight planets.

EARTH

Earth is the middle-sized planet. Four of the nine planets are smaller and four are bigger than planet Earth.

MARS

Mars has a very large canyon. It is the biggest in the solar system. It is called Mariner Valley and is thirteen times longer than the Grand Canyon in the United States.

JUPITER

Jupiter is huge! If Jupiter were a big, empty ball, more than one thousand Earths would fill it.

SATURN

It is very windy on Saturn. Around its middle, winds blow ten times stronger than an average hurricane on Earth.

URANUS

When the spacecraft *Voyager II* flew past Uranus in 1986, it had been traveling through space for 9 years.

NEPTUNE

Neptune is thirty times Earth's distance from the sun. Some astronomers have said that studying Neptune from Earth is like studying a dime a mile away.

PLUTO

Pluto is the only planet that has never been explored by a spacecraft.

An ASTRONOMER is someone who studies the stars and planets.

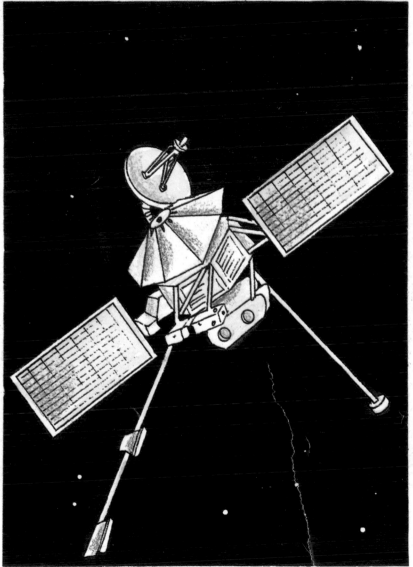

Here on planet Earth, astronomers search the skies through telescopes. Spacecraft are sent into the solar system and beyond in search of new discoveries.

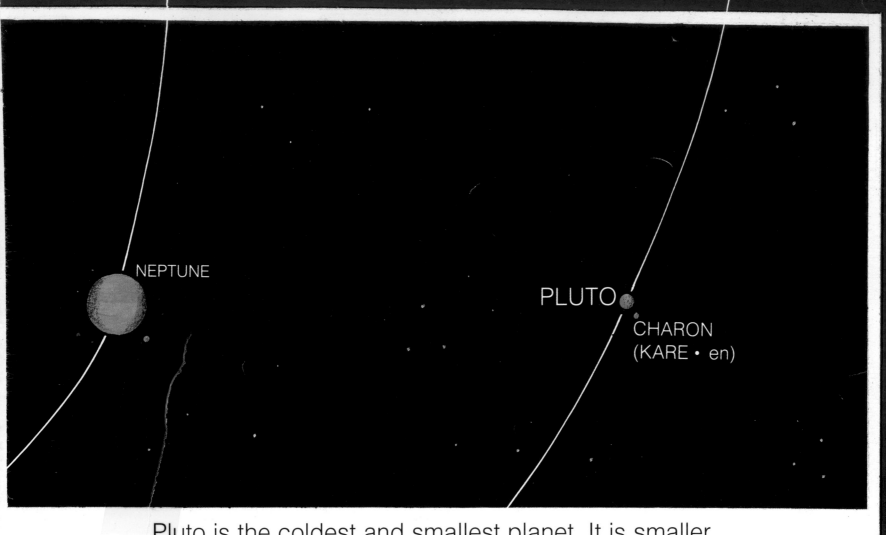

Pluto is the coldest and smallest planet. It is smaller than Earth's moon. It has one moon called Charon. One year on Pluto is about 248 Earth years long. A day on Pluto is about 6 Earth days long.

PLUTO

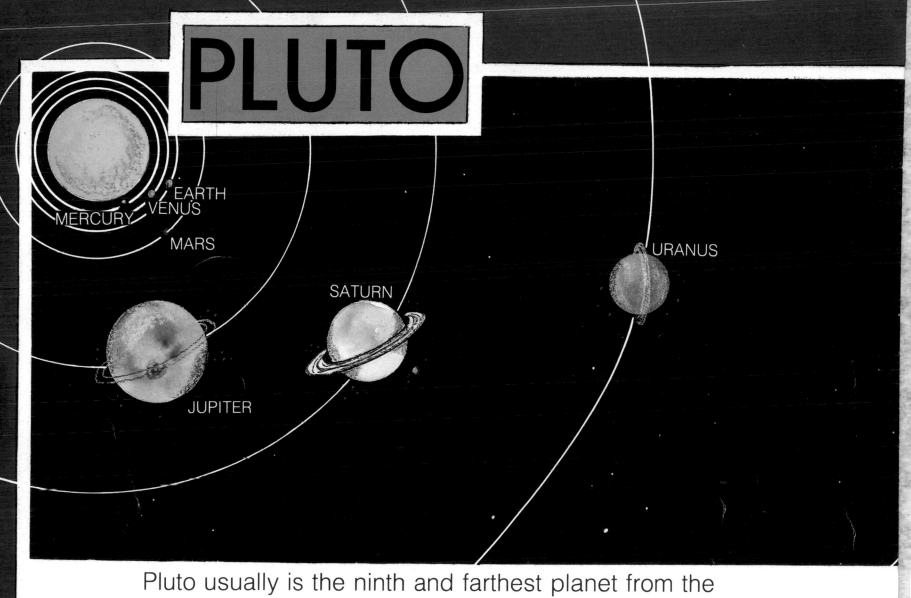

MERCURY
VENUS
EARTH
MARS
JUPITER
SATURN
URANUS

Pluto usually is the ninth and farthest planet from the sun. Sometimes its orbit carries it closer to the sun than Neptune. At its farthest, Pluto is about 3.6 billion miles from the sun. It was discovered in 1930.

NEPTUNE

TRITON
(TRITE • n)

VOYAGER II

One of Neptune's thirteen moons, Triton, is about the same size as planet Earth's moon. The spacecraft *Voyager II* visited Neptune in 1989. One Neptune year is 164 Earth years. It rotates in about 16 Earth hours.

NEPTUNE

MERCURY
VENUS
EARTH
MARS
JUPITER
SATURN
URANUS
NEPTUNE

Neptune is the eighth farthest planet from the sun. It is about 2.8 billion miles away. Neptune appears to be blue because of a gas in its atmosphere. It is almost the same size as Uranus.

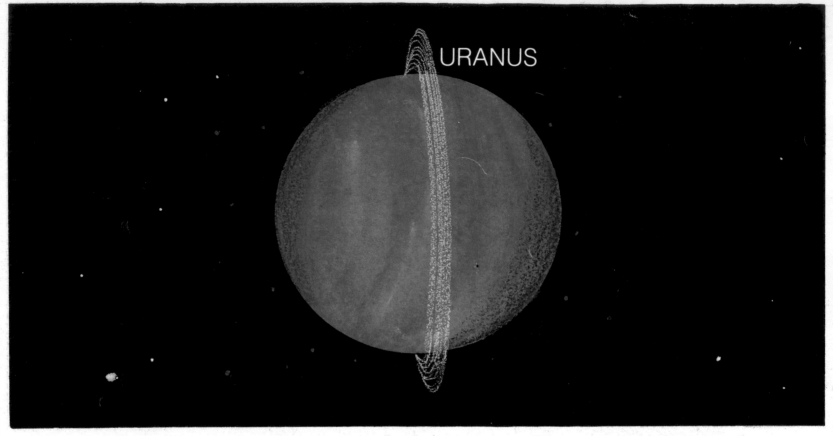

URANUS

Uranus is the third biggest planet, about one-third the size of planet Jupiter. At least twenty-seven moons orbit around it. Planets farther from the sun have longer orbits. They take more time to travel around the sun. For Uranus to make one orbit takes about 84 Earth years. Uranus rotates in about 17 Earth hours.

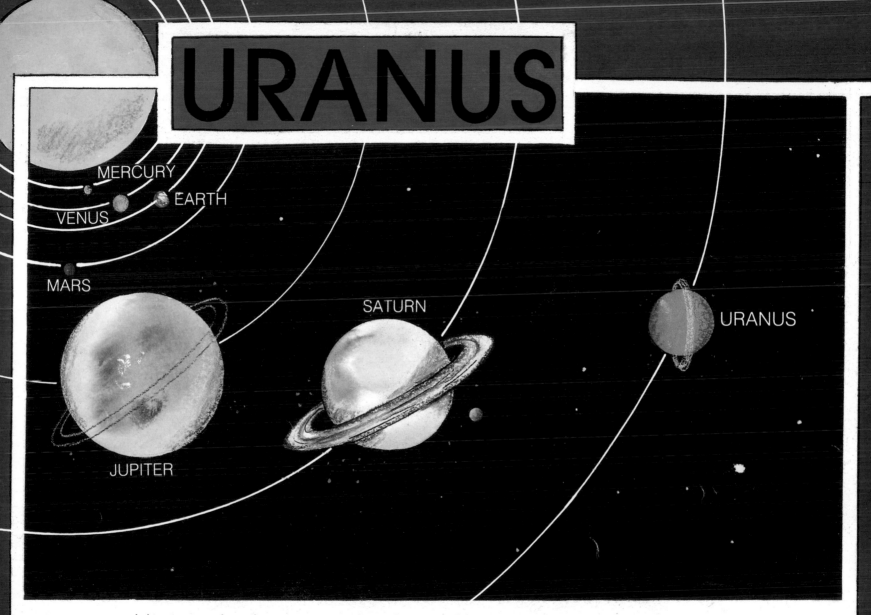

URANUS

Uranus is the seventh planet from the sun. It is about 1.8 billion miles away. It is so far away that from its surface the sun would look tiny. Uranus has ten rings.

SATURN

TITAN
(TITE · n)

Saturn has at least forty-six moons. Titan, its largest
moon, is the only moon in the solar system with an
atmosphere and clouds. It takes almost 30 Earth
years for Saturn to orbit the sun. It rotates in about
11 Earth hours.

SATURN

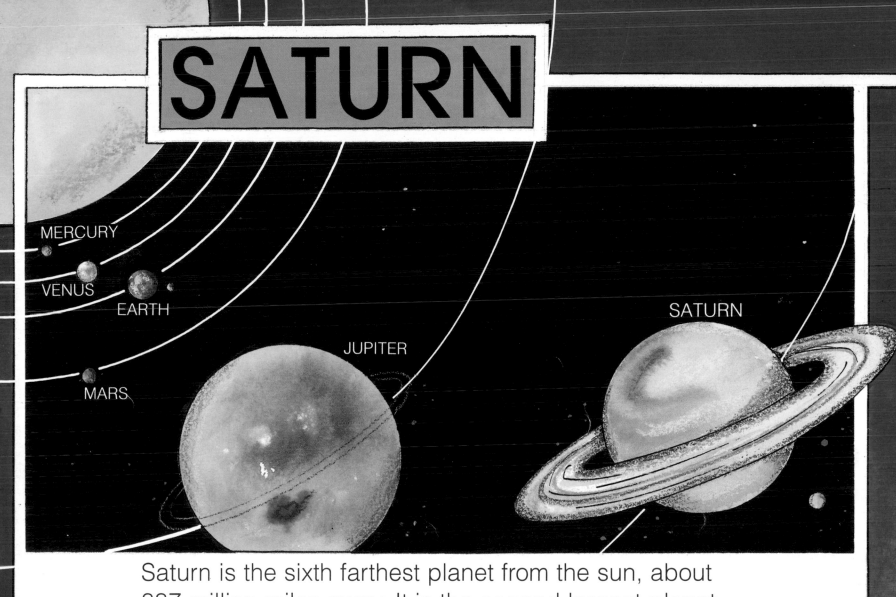

MERCURY

VENUS

EARTH

MARS

JUPITER

SATURN

Saturn is the sixth farthest planet from the sun, about 887 million miles away. It is the second largest planet. Saturn's hundreds of rings make it look different from the other planets. The rings are made up of ice. Some pieces are as big as houses. On Saturn it is extremely cold.

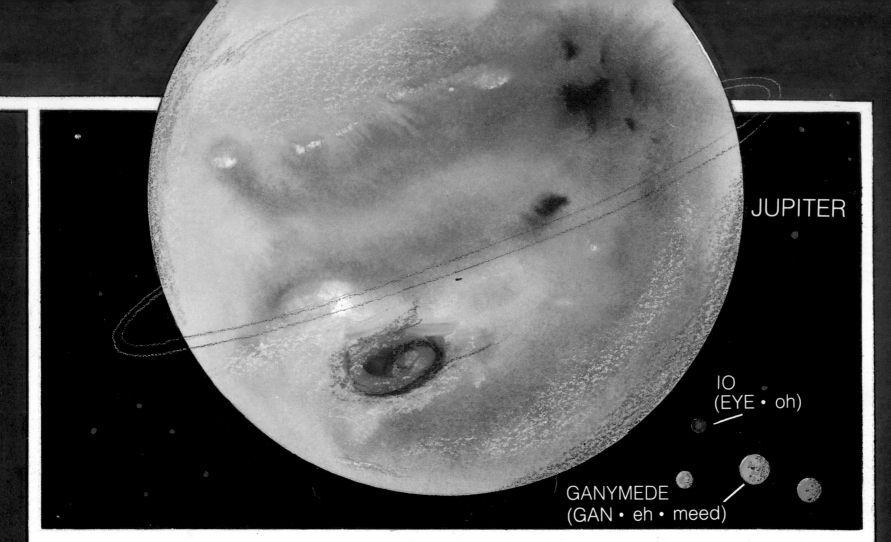

JUPITER

IO
(EYE • oh)

GANYMEDE
(GAN • eh • meed)

At least sixty-three moons orbit around planet Jupiter.
One moon, Ganymede, is the biggest moon in the solar
system. It is bigger than planet Mercury. Another moon,
called Io, has many active volcanoes. One Jupiter year
is almost 12 Earth years. It has short days, just under
10 Earth hours long.

JUPITER

MERCURY

VENUS

EARTH

MARS

JUPITER

RINGS
are made up of rock,
bits of ice
and dust.

GREAT RED SPOT

Jupiter is the fifth planet from the sun. It is about 484 million miles away. It is huge! It is bigger than all the other planets put together and has rings. Jupiter is mostly made up of gases. Some of the gases form a giant red circle called the Great Red Spot.

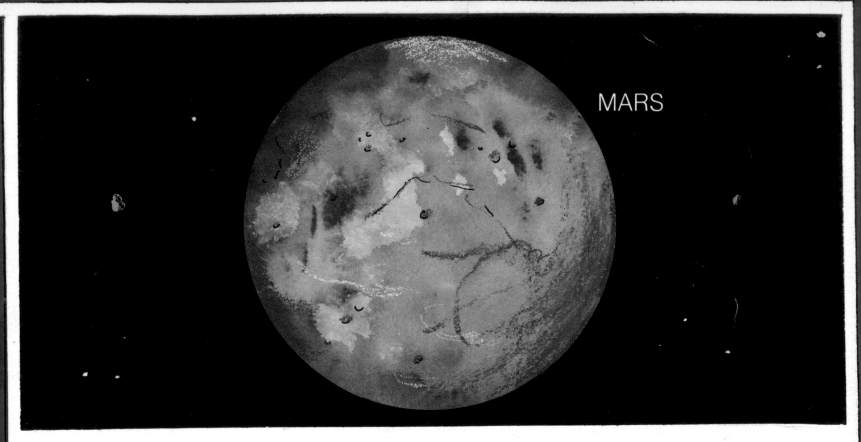

MARS

Astronomers believe that Mars looks red because iron on its surface has been rusted by the planet's thin atmosphere. It is very cold and is a little more than half the size of planet Earth. Mars has two small moons. One year on Mars is about 2 Earth years. A day on Mars is about as long as a day on Earth.

MARS

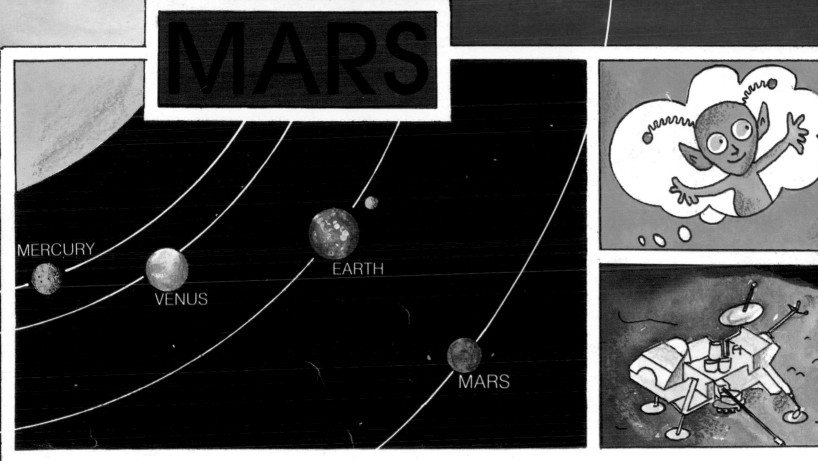

MERCURY

VENUS

EARTH

MARS

Mars is the fourth planet from the sun, about 142 million miles away. People wonder if there was ever life on Mars. Although the surface of Mars is dry now, it once had rivers and perhaps even an ocean. In 2004, the Mars Exploration Rover Mission sent two robotic vehicles to examine the planet's surface. Scientists may still find evidence of life-forms.

A MOON orbits a planet. It has no light of its own. It reflects sunlight.

EARTH

GRAVITY pulls things toward Earth.

VENUS

MERCURY

Planet Earth has just enough gravity to hold its atmosphere around it. Earth has a moon. The moon causes the tides to change, making them rise and fall. Earth orbits the sun in about 365 days to make an Earth year. It rotates every 24 hours to make an Earth day.

EARTH

Earth is the third planet from the sun. It is the only planet known to have just the right environment for plants, animals, and people to live in. Earth is 93 million miles from the sun.

Venus is about 67 million miles away from the sun. It is hot there. Venus is almost the same size as planet Earth. One year on Venus is about 225 Earth days. A day on Venus is about 243 Earth days long because Venus rotates very slowly. On Venus, a day is longer than a year, and a year is shorter than a day.

VENUS

VENUS

Venus is the second planet from the sun. It is usually the brightest object in our sky, other than our sun and moon. At sunrise and sunset, it looks like a big, bright star. It is bright because Venus has a cloud cover that reflects the sunlight. These clouds are made up of gases.

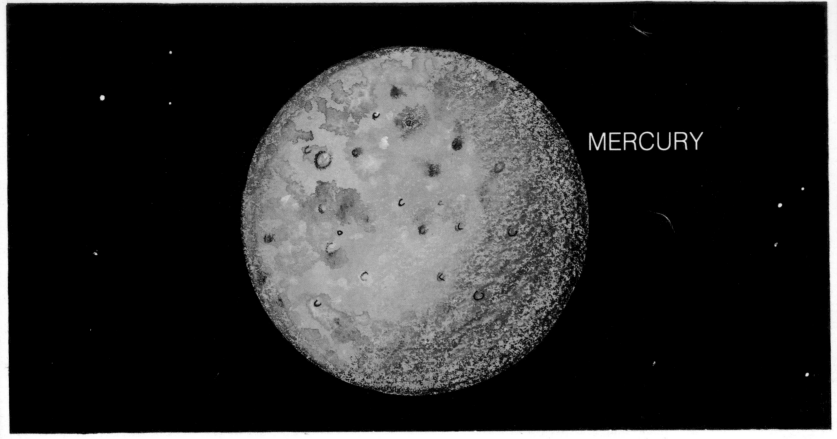

MERCURY

Mercury is the second smallest planet of the nine planets and is made up of rock and metal. One year on Mercury is only 88 Earth days. That's how long it takes for Mercury to orbit the sun. Mercury rotates very slowly, so its days are very long. A day on Mercury is 59 Earth days.

MERCURY

An ATMOSPHERE is
a layer of air.

MERCURY

Of the nine planets, Mercury is the planet closest to
the sun. It is about 36 million miles away from the sun.
During the day it is extremely hot. During the night it
is bitter cold because Mercury doesn't have any
atmosphere to keep its heat from escaping.

A TELESCOPE enlarges the image.

People can look up on a clear night and might see Mercury, Venus, Mars, Jupiter, and Saturn. A planet looks like a steady point of light. A star twinkles. A telescope is needed to see Uranus, Neptune, and Pluto. They are very far away from planet Earth.

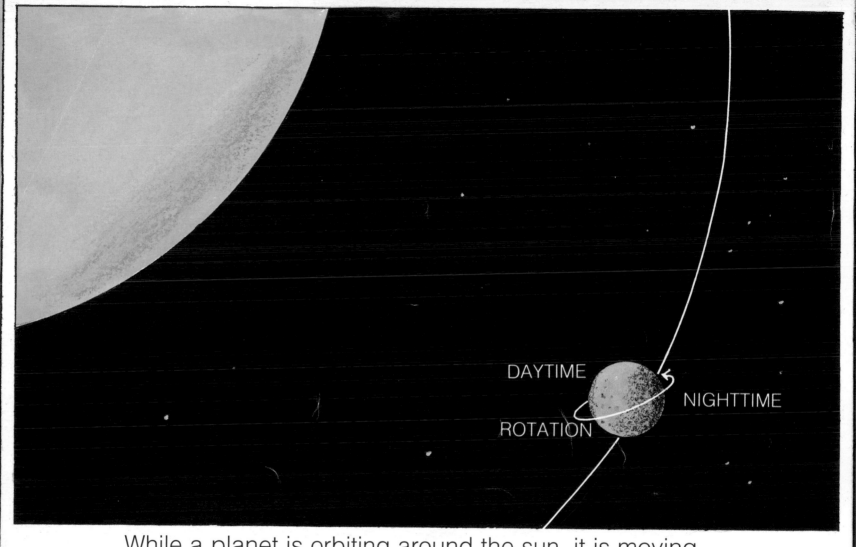

DAYTIME

NIGHTTIME

ROTATION

While a planet is orbiting around the sun, it is moving another way, too. It spins, or rotates. The time it takes for a planet to rotate is its day. Each planet's day is different. While a planet is rotating, part of it faces the sun. It is daytime there. On the other side it is nighttime.

The nine planets circle around the sun in paths called orbits. The time it takes for a planet to travel around the sun is its year. Each planet's year is different.

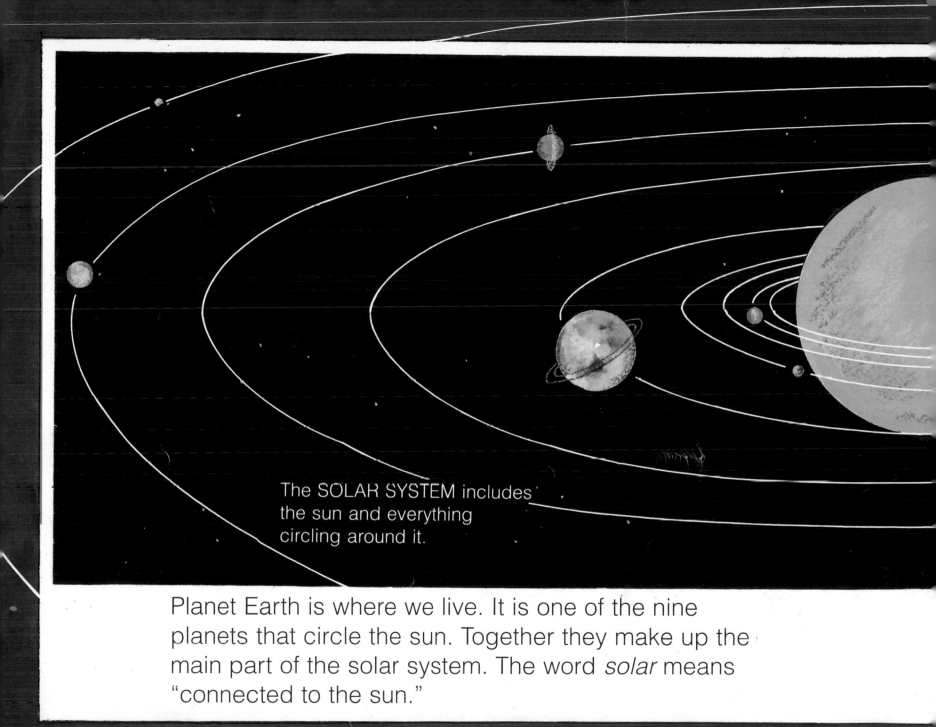

The SOLAR SYSTEM includes
the sun and everything
circling around it.

Planet Earth is where we live. It is one of the nine
planets that circle the sun. Together they make up the
main part of the solar system. The word *solar* means
"connected to the sun."

In very early times, people knew of six planets. They were Mercury, Venus, Earth, Mars, Jupiter, and Saturn. These people named the planets after Greek and Roman goddesses and gods. Later, within the last 200 years, three more were discovered. They are Uranus, Neptune, and Pluto.

A planet is different from a star. People can see a planet because the sun shines on it. A star shines because it is made up of gases that give off light and heat. Our sun is a star. Nearly every star is much bigger than the biggest planet.

PLANET

On a clear night, when stars shine brightly, you might see what looks like another star. But each night it changes position in the star patterns. It is a planet. The word *planet* comes from the Greek word meaning "wanderer."

For Charlie Pratt

Special thanks to Professor Edward Foley, teacher of
astronomy, St. Michael's College, Colchester, Vermont,
and David Hogenboom, Professor Emeritus of Astronomy,
Lafayette College, Easton, Pennsylvania

Library of Congress Cataloging-in-Publication Data
Gibbons, Gail.
    The planets / by Gail Gibbons.
        Rev. ed.   p.   cm.
    ISBN 0-8234-1957-6 (hardcover)
    ISBN 0-8234-1958-4 (paperback)
    1. Planets—Juvenile literature. [1. Planets.] I. Title.
    QB602.G53   2005   92-44429 CIP   AC
    523.4—dc20

    ISBN-13: 978-0-8234-1957-9 (hardcover)
    ISBN-13: 978-0-8234-1958-6 (paperback)

    ISBN-10: 0-8234-1957-6 (hardcover)
    ISBN-10: 0-8234-1958-4 (paperback)

PLUTO

URANUS

NEPTUNE

VENUS

MARS

JUPITER

THE PLANETS

REVISED EDITION

By GAIL GIBBONS

HOLIDAY HOUSE · NEW YORK

MOUNT PLEASANT